The Comic Flaw

The Comic Flaw

poems by
Alan Berecka

Foreword by
Angela Alaimo O'Donnell

neoNuma
A R T S
HOUSTON, TX

neoNuma Arts
P.O. Box 460248
Houston, TX 77056

www.neonuma.com

Library of Congress Control Number: 2008942632

ISBN: 978-0-9741623-6-2

Author's Note

Many thanks to all those who have given their time in preparation of these poems and this manuscript, especially, Neil Orts, Larry Thomas, Barbara Crooker, Angela O'Donnell, Jill Alexander Essbaum, Steven Schroeder, Rick Sale, Leslie Palmer, Scott Cairns, Brigit Pegeen Kelly, B.H. Fairchild, David Stringer, Yucatan Rodrigues, Don Wall, Sara Kaplan, Doug Jordan, Audell Shelburne, and the members of the Corpus Christi Writers Circle.

Also many thanks to my parents Albert and Stella Berecka for giving me a unique childhood that I learn to appreciate more each day, to my sister Janis for introducing poetry to our childhood home, to the Graves family for years of support, to Alice, Rachael, and Aaron for their constant love of this flawed man.

Contents

Comic Spirit(s)

ALAN BERECKA'S FIRST BOOK OF POEMS begins and ends in dreams. The first poem takes place on a pier as his great-grandfather disembarks from a boat just arrived from "the old country." Un-bound by time and dis-placed in space, the poet holds parlance with the dead, urging Piusus Antonavage to return to the world to which he belongs as life on this shore will prove hard and poor. The old man drinks a long glass of beer, grins, and responds wryly: "Each man has one life. What does it matter where he breeds or drinks?"

A question for the ages, indeed, and one that haunts this volume, though a happy haunting it is. In the pages that follow, there is much drinking and breeding, most of it carried out with grit and gusto by Berecka's family members, who are just as colorful and just as plain-dealing as old Piusus himself. These include the likes of a card-sharp grandmother, a mad aunt who believes herself a cow, an "idiot uncle" who drops his birthday cake and lives his (many) remaining years in terror of the premature death portended, a hardworking and harder-drinking father, and a saintly mother who suffers through it all. These people, most of them passed, or fast-passing, out of this life, are very much alive in Berecka's book. They move across the pages like muchloved, holy ghosts, all conjured by the poet, who serves as affable Polish-Lithuanian-American spirit medium who seems glad for the company. As for the lucky reader, he or she is rapt by story after story, ranging from the riotous to the merely merry, for the spirit that presides over all the others is that of Comedy herself, wise and winsome in her ways, a blessed presence who makes life bearable and art possible.

Berecka's gifts as a narrative poet are many. Among these is his capacity for the gently grotesque. These poems often relate scenes and events that are sad, and even tragic, in their implications. A drunken father polkas around the dance floor, his small son clutched to his chest like a pigskin football; the same father, described as "a masked alien master / of fire, heat, and light, the violator / of cold elements," wakes his sleeping children and drives them across mountain roads to see the ruined, rusted remains of one of his creations; the same father flees his wife, with his son in tow, to spend Saturday drinking and swearing with cronies, hides pornography in his sock drawer, and, cast as "a bull of a man" wielding a "razor strop," punishes his son for his childhood transgressions. Berecka does not flinch from the reality of life growing up amid this deeply flawed family, yet always insists upon tempering judgment with generosity—a generosity that manifests itself in wit and wordplay, in the blending of unexpected grace with ordinary failure, in representing the paradox of human error governed by love. In the title poem of the volume, the poet asks the keynote question: if "I can't laugh at my childhood, /what am I supposed to do with it?" True to the ethos of Comedy, Berecka absolves each and all for their sins and holds out the possibility for them to become their better selves.

Such forgiveness is based in Comedy and also in the faith passed on to Berecka by his parents and grandparents, Roman Catholics with an Eastern European flavor strong as sauerkraut. The poet renders much of his religious formation with characteristic humor: the child's nightly fear of not "signing off" properly ("Father, Son, Holy Ghost") before dropping off to sleep, his fanciful conflation of the four-foot-high-replica of the crucified Christ hanging in his church with a similarly sized poster of Carl Yaztremski on his bedroom wall, the buzz—and inevitable guilt—from stolen sips of communion wine. This is the universal stuff of a Catholic Childhood—albeit seen and narrated from Berecka's skewed perspective—which resonates and delights. Yet, ultimately, the poet's comic vision is grounded in a serious theology: the belief in the goodness of God and of the creation, made manifest again and again in the human beings who have graced his life and shaped his generous vision. Berecka's faith is neither pious nor easy: he loses and finds it, loves and loathes it, wrestles with it, and passes it on to his own children. In all these stages of (un)belief, the language and imagery of sacramentality—sacraments as visible signs of what exists but cannot be seen—pervades these poems as surely as they pervade the poet's consciousness. This is especially poignant in his poems about his own family, his wife and children. The words he writes for his daughter as she leaves home for college become Eucharist—pieces of his heart embedded in his art—his body, his blood, offered to his child.

The final poem of *The Comic Flaw* returns us, once again, to the realm of dreams. As with old Piusus, the poet finds himself speaking to the dead—one last genial ghost who haunts the volume—this time, the old

Lithuanian priest under whose strict guidance the young poet had served as altar boy. During the Easter Vigil, long ago, the priest died suddenly on the altar, initiating the child into the adult nightmare of existential terror. Now, mercifully, 30 years later, the poet dreams the old man alive, who comes to him offering two chalices filled with wine. In sacramental gesture that looks forward as well as back, uniting Berecka's ancestral past with his Providential future, the priest issues a simple invitation: "There's plenty. Let's drink." Berecka's received faith and native disposition merge and mingle here, in these cups of wine. In defiance of his boyhood fears, death gives way to life, and the Christian vision manifests itself as ultimately Comic, with Christ as King of the Comedy.

These poems offer all these gifts—and more—extending to the reader the glass of beer, the cup of wine, along with the poet's own invitation to the Eucharistic feast. Here, he says: "There's plenty. Let's drink."

Choose your cup. Drink deep.

Angela Alaimo O'Donnell
Fordham University
New York City
All Souls' Day, 2008

An American Dreams

I stand waiting as Piusus Antonavage,
my great-grandfather, young, fresh
from the old country disembarks.
I find him on the pier, tired and gray,
smelling of cabbage and onions
being coerced toward customs
with little to declare.

With a large shepherd's crook,
I cut him from the flock
and plead with him to return
to where he belongs, where he
has always belonged. I tell him
no matter what he wants, he will father
an eloigned race. I plead with him
not to make this mistake.

His blue eyes, deep set, bleed
with rage. *You whiney bastard,*
belong to what? There I have nothing
but starving mouths I cannot feed.

The cane now raised in his hands
becomes a giant red serpent.
Growing, its coils anchor my feet.

Weeks pass. He comes to me again.
This time I walk with my grandmother,
both of us children. We carry a bucket of beer
and change back from the corner joint. He sits
on a bright white porch where children play
at captaining ships. He pours a glass, drinks
deeply and grins. In a thinning accent he tells me,
Boy, it is not so good to think so much.
What is there to know? Each man has one life.
What does it matter where he breeds or drinks?

A Modest Proposal

When the legend becomes fact, print the legend.
The Man Who Shot Liberty Valance

She enjoyed playing hard to get. When he
had arrived, after a morning spent aboard
the train from Amsterdam, she was unimpressed
by this bald man who was much older
and shorter than she. But then she was taken
by his wit, facets of which sparked her eyes.
At the end of the formal date in her parents'
parlor, they shook hands and promised to write.

And they did. Their letters grew long,
then longer, as she began to grow attached
to the idea of having intelligent children,
unlike the thick kids that she was aunt to.

She courted like she played pinochle—she kept
her cards close to her chest. In the second year
near Christmas when he proposed in longhand,
she answered coolly, *Should you return to Utica*
and ask me in person, I might consider the matter.

For years she was pleased to have made him sweat,
but as their five children began to age, she learned
why they call wit sharp. *Dad how did you meet*
mother? It was a question her clever mate
loved to answer. *I had come to Utica on business.*
At the corner of Genesee and Bleeker, I saw
a young woman. She was not bad looking,
but she was crying. So I asked her, Miss
what's wrong? She replied, I am nineteen
and no one will marry me. I looked at her
one more time and said, Stop crying.

She could have burnt all those letters
she saved. For now, three generations later
she's known as the bride who dried her eyes.

My Week as an Illegal Alien
para mis hermanos y hermanas

When I was a kid, Great Uncle Billy
let slip the family secret—his father,
Piusus Antonavage, was a wetback.
Unable to get into America
through Ellis Island, the bullheaded Litvok
went north and then snuck in from Canada
crawling along the underside of a railway
trestle that spanned the St. Lawrence.

When I learned of my illegal roots,
I feared the worst and the INS
who upon finding out, would no doubt
deport us, the descendants of an ancient
crime, back to Lithuania, back behind
the iron curtain where gray people
never smiled, never prayed, never played
baseball, and only ate borscht and boiled cabbage.

The fear festered for days until my mom,
who constantly studied the barometer
of her moody son's dispositions, asked
me what had caused my current low to form.

Confronted, I confessed that I did not want
to be sent back to the old country and its older
ways. My mother who spoke no English
until she was old enough to go to school,
the daughter of two legal Polish immigrants,
laughed. She said, *Let me get this straight.
You're worried because no one checked
your great-grandfather's papers?* I nodded.
Son, relax. No one checked the Pilgrims' either.

3

My Father's Dance

My father never waltzed. He polkaed,
while leading a life too unrefined
for three-quarter time.

Near the end of every church hall dance
just before last call, he hoisted me up
to his beer barrel chest, where I bathed
in ninety proof, his eyes and mine forced
half shut by a charred filter that burned
beneath an arc of ash. It balanced magically
on his thin jutted lip. My hand vanished
past the wrist, enveloped by his beaten
tin-knocker's grip, my weak arm pulled stiff
into the Heisman pose. I became the small
cotton pigskin, the kind carried to daylight
by plastic backs on electronic gridirons.
We bounded, juking in concentric paths, riding
the vibrations of a Polish tune until the part-time
musicians packed up their accordions and clarinets.

Our dance done, my dad stowed me on a cold metal
chair where I curled and slept while my mother
helped with the dishes, and my father swept
sawdust and cigarette butts into a large dustpan.

The Life of a Cricket

No request is too extreme...
"*When You Wish Upon a Star,*" *Ned Washington*

Early on Saturdays, once the husband
had mowed or raked the yard
or shoveled the drive, he informed

his wife that he was going to town
to buy supplies, or visit his mother, or help
his brother. He announced his departure

as he neared the kitchen door. *But lunch
is nearly cooked,* the woman countered
standing stove-side. *No problem, an hour*

tops. He replied in stride, hoping to grab
and turn the brass knob. *Fine one hour,
then take the kid. He needs to get out.*

She stood there stirring the pot
raising her stained wooden spoon—
a magic wand that stopped

her fleeing mate cold in his tracks.
*Ah, Ma how come I gotta? Because
it's only an hour, go keep your father*

company. With her trump card played,
the husband's only way out was to call
her bluff. *OK kid, let's go. Remember*

it's her idea. The errand never took long.
Then they'd cruise the east side, circling,
hunting for the cars of the dad's union

brothers, boyhood friends, or even shoe-string
relatives parked near a corner beer joint.
There was always someone inside Gideon's

or Stromboli's, so he'd pull to the curb.
Time enough for a quick one. Hand-in-hand
the AWOL dad and his pint-sized sidekick

pushed on into a smoke-filled dimly-lit din.
The kid would be hoisted onto a chrome and leather
stool, from where he'd be schooled that when you sit

in a bar, it makes no difference who you are,
there are rules that men drink and live by.
The new guy must buy the next round

and then be repaid in kind. A drunken
Ponzi scheme, an accountant's nightmare,
that could continue until last call. It restarted

every time someone known and sober stumbled
in. One beer could lead to a dozen. Only
the cheapest of SOBs would leave owing

someone else a brew. On his perch the boy
was fed peanuts and potato chips which he
washed down with Coca-Colas and orange Nehis

served over ice in large pilsner glasses.
The kid strained to hear that day's televised
game over the men's complaints about family ties

or jackasses like their foremen or in-laws.
The boy bided his time, waiting for the men's speech
to slur and turn bluer, then he would begin to beg

for quarters, so he could escape to the corner
where the bar's amusements stood idle.
He fed his coins into pinball and shuffle bowling

machines. Three games for a quarter,
he learned to pace himself, to hold the ball
on the flipper, prolonging his escape

into the field of bells, flashing lights and spinning
numbers, but even if he won a game or two,
the boy knew he would need to return and sit

until, just as hope faded, some *blue-balled fairy*
might finally look at his watch and mutter, *Damn,*

will you look at the time! I'm gonna catch

hell, so I better get going. The other men
would vent—*Pussy whipped. Jackass. Asshole.*
But once the pyramid scheme broke, time turned

real. Soon the father, son in tow, staggered back
out into the night. They piled into their whale
of a sedan, hoping to find their way home

behind a set of high-beaming headlights
that swerved madly like prison beacons
tracking escaped felons, until the fugitives

reentered the once fled kitchen. *One hour!*
Where the hell have you been. Oh Christ,
never mind. She bent down to wipe

the orange mustache off her son's face
while the father slurped cold stew
with a fluttering hand. He explained

that a man just can't leave, but she never
understood how could he take a kid into a bar,
no matter, at least her conscience was clean.

Initiation

Between my finger and my thumb the squat pen rests.
"Digging," Seamus Heaney

Years later I sit plying this clean
craft, fusing words and metaphors—
trying to approximate the form
of what I now know was nothing
more than a giant sawdust collector.

My father welded—a masked alien master
of fire, heat, and light, the violator
of cold elements—contorting, torturing
rigid steel until it satisfied his designs.

Hephaestus unmasked returned
home each weekday night,
dressed in thick green sweat-stained
cotton. At the kitchen table he sat
burnt, cut, unlacing his boots
while supper and beer appeared
before him. He transformed,
slumping back into his human form—
a silent keeper of the mysteries
of his trade and flame.

Deep in the mountains, he roused
us early from our tent. That summer's
Adirondack lake would have to wait.
In his old Rambler wagon, we cruised
into an unknown town. Hungry hoping
for food, my disappointment grew
as we drove past an open diner
and finally onto the grounds of what he said
was a bowling pin factory. We parked
and began to walk across its grounds.
Stuck on unamused, my mood turned,
as we rounded the corner of some building
and there it stood—a stainless colossus,
an earthbound Saturn pointing
at the light-blue morning moon,
sitting at t-minus five and counting.

We stood there silently, my head
near his belt until he pointed
a bandaged finger in the air
and said, *There. I built that.*

Educational TV

Behind her camera, behind the flash,
my nearly nubile sister sat enrapt,
her tears blurring her view
finder as she popped bulb after bulb
shooting the Beatles on *Ed Sullivan,*
received live on our old black and white TV.

Something had changed when she
heard them on her transistor radio.
Now she watched them, and they were more
than just standing there. She ignored
the screams that drowned their songs.
She understood the need. Besides,
the band's 45s could be bought,
but soon she would own their faces,
instamatic icons of Paul and George,
relics for her pre-teen devotion.

She had saved, paid in full for the film.
To pay for its development, she promised
that she would not only wash, but dry
the family's dishes for an entire month.

The photos took forever, but one night
my father returned from work
with a yellow and red Kodak
bag stowed in his tin lunch box.
My sister, brimming with passion,
tore into the envelope. She scanned
the first few shots, her eyes searching
wildly, turned red, then filled with panic
as she fumbled through the stack.
Bawling, she hurled the photos
against the kitchen wall, sprinted down
the hall, slammed her bedroom door.

My mother gave chase. My father
cursed. I began to collect
the strewn exposures from the floor.
Each picture a photographic clone,
born in her flawed belief that she

could capture a flicker of light
with the wrong shutter speed,
an entire roll of the same shot—
an oaken cabinet and its blank screen.

The Oracle's Art

Aunt Julia loved to snap photographs.
Normally mouse-like, she dominated
family gatherings—demanding cheese
from those she trapped and lined up
to pose against a wall, to be shot
by her solar flash. She executed
her art until our rooms filled
with the glow of floating blue dots.

With her developed film, she traveled
the family circuit to show off her exposures.
When she visited us, we sat in a line
on our long brown couch, knowing
before she opened her drug store envelope
that we were about to see badly skewed
and off-centered photos of shoes, knees,
headless shirts, beer bellies in stretched
sweaters, and the occasional blurred ear lobe.
We tried not to laugh as Julia, sitting
on the sofa's center cushion, told us
in all her seriousness what each photo
really showed—how each of our missed
faces looked, what we thought, how we felt.

The Last Laugh

Armed with my Daisy Winchester
filled with BBs, I left the house
with a friend from the neighborhood—
preteens on the prowl looking
for something to kill. We went down
to the Nine Mile Creek, to a cold
deep pool filled with slow fat frogs.

We aimed for their heads—
splitting skulls, piercing brains.
We became Lee and Harvey,
the Oswald twins.

I forget what ran out first,
the frogs or our ammo. I left
for home feeling grownup,
like my uncle who hunted
deer and would appear
in our driveway, smiling
while showing off some gunned-
down buck—gutted and roped
to the blood-splattered roof
of his rusted station wagon.

That night after I hunkered
down in bed, I closed my eyes,
only to rerun my last kill. I watched
as it tried to swim off, getting just
about out of range, when I shot
and nailed the back of its head.
In death the frog spun and stared
with large blank eyes, a smirk
on its alien face, as the corpse
began to sink. I followed it down.
The grin grew to a sick smile
that held me fast, until we fell
through the murk and into the cold
black that's found six feet down.

Spontaneous Combustion

The strange alchemy
which transforms water
into fire is nothing more
than the common chemistry
of a dairy farmer's error.

Moisture, traces of heavy
dews and summer rains,
trapped deep inside a tightly
bound bail of still green hay
buried deep inside a mow
will dry deep in that darkness
creating its own heat,
and like a madman's genius
long suppressed and compressed,
it will spark—deep
inside at first, a smoldering heat
that seeks to consume its darkness
until it can feed openly and rage
becoming an unforgiving blaze.

Everyday at noon
the fire whistle blew,
just a test, a piece
of the rural landscape
that we all knew.

When it blew off schedule,
my father, who never volunteered
for anything, scanned the valley
from his backyard view,
and as other men raced to the firehouse
in rusted pickups, portable blue
lights flashing, my father sought the smoke.
Binoculars in hand, he circled, a human
pointer on the scent, until he'd give up
the hunt or find a distant black plume.
Then arms and tongue wagging, he'd herd
us into the old blue four-door Malibu
and using the smoke as a guide, he'd drive
until we'd reach a distant farm, barn

red hot, circled by chaos and firemen
from half the county, containing
more than extinguishing,
keeping the house roof wet,
wrestling livestock from the heat,
and then he'd park along the road,
and we would watch using the car's trunk
and hood as our seats. We settled in,
part of an audience that would stretch
down and up the road for fifty car lengths
or so. Some bystanders would wander
from car to car seeking news, spreading rumors.
Others screamed tired jokes, *I like my beef
well-done,* but mostly everyone watched
and groused about the volunteers
until the barn would burn itself out.
Then we'd all climb back into our rides,
and headlights on, begin the drive home.

Once the second cut of hay was stowed,
my life settled back into long evenings
spent listening to Rizutto calling Yankee
games and screaming *Holy cow!*
out of a cheap transistor radio
while I watched reruns in black and white.

When the special issue of *TV Guide,*
the one that promised new hit shows,
came home from town with the rest
of the groceries, it meant my life
would soon turn into an endless bus
ride between home and a remote school.

An early stop on the route, I sat
by a window, behind the driver,
halfway back. On the way to the first
day of the fifth grade, the bus slowed
then stopped for the two girls
who stood in front of a burnt out barn.
Once they took their seat, the one in front
of mine, the bus moved on. They began
to answer questions, about their parents
who had begun to look for work, about plans

to rebuild someday, about how the cows
had to be sold, about how their lives had changed.

I had nothing to ask. Suddenly overcome
by the stench of Naugahyde, I sat sweating,
my head pressed to cold glass and learned
a lesson my old man never got—
the sudden burn of empathy.

Child Rearing

*Just wait until your father
gets home.* An unwelcomed
mantra the boy's mother sung
often after his boyhood
transgressions were judged
too great for the metal end
of the fly swatter that hung
next to the bathroom door.

Banished to his bed,
the boy just waited
for the father's return
and aged long years
each hour, as he waited
to hear crushed gravel groan
under the weight of braking tires,
waited for a rusted car door
to fall shut, waited for a garage
door to rumble open, waited
for the report of a the father's tin
lunch pail against a screen door,
waited for the first heavy footfall
on the cold linoleum, waited
for the shrill question muted
by a houseful of walls, *Do you
know what your son did today?*

*Jeezus Key-riste woman
don't start with me now,*
the father's often ignored reply
went unnoticed as she repeated
the boy's trespasses with the zeal
of an Old Testament prophet.

The wait was over.
The father appeared, a bull of a man
dressed in green denim and sweat,
while the boy stared at the right hand
of the father, which held the razor strop.
Once used by earlier generations
in an older country to hone

precision into a tailor's tools,
now it would serve to sharpen
a wayward boy's moral acumen.

With little enthusiasm
and less eye contact, the father
said, *Let's get this done.*
The boy rolled obediently
onto his stomach and was stung
until all had been paid in full.

On those nights supper was served
and consumed in a forced silence
which the father chased down
with a few extra beers.
Later, as the family stared
at the black and white TV, the balance
seemed to return to their communal lives
as if some sacrifice had made things right.

Cleaned Ice

He always stopped the show, wide and big-boned
with a bald, bristled, many-chinned head.
He always chewed the same cigar's end
beneath his large red bulbous nose.
He never grinned, cared little for fashion
wearing black rubbers over his work boots.
He was past old. I knew that if he
belched it would smell of beer and pickled eggs.
Standing as he worked, he moved one hand.
He drove the Zamboni. I hated him.

From my nosebleed seat, I waited
for him to misjudge a corner, spin, bang
the boards, knocking the end screens out
of place. When he did, I'd clap and hoot
Hey, Jerkface, them's the brakes! He
never looked up, but an old usher always did.
I slunk low in my chair, and prayed that Dad
would get back with my Coke and his beer.

Once the Eastern Hockey League could draw large
rowdy crowds, when the major league clubs
were too few, and the minors were for all the less
than greats and those older than great. Oh, they
were good, just not good enough to escape, so they
laced their skates for drunken construction workers,
zitted teenagers on the prowl, bored women
on soon-to-be-forgotten dates
and us—sons of all the above.   .

They were Armstrong, Anderson, Bannerman, Hook,
Babando, Kane, Kelly, Babiuk, Speck and Smith—
star members of the Clinton Comets and small town lore.
I remember their goals, their saves, their fights,
and their blood that stained the auditorium's ice.

The Zamboni erased it all
with its slow and steady swipes.

The Naked Truth

I knew where those women hid. I found
them that time my mother sent me
to stow her mate's just-washed underwear
into his top dresser drawer, and there beneath
his last pair of clean briefs, I caught a glimpse
of a glossy cover. A nearly naked temptress
beckoned to me, *Don't be shy. Turn the page.*

I had no idea what I'd find there, but I would learn
with every chance I got to return. I memorized
their curves, rolls, shadows, and even their names.
I feared the possibility of parental footfalls, so I stood
there dumbly, numb like Adam did that day
he realized that he was naked but so was Eve—
that moment when shame first mated desire.

It's the Giving that Counts

...he will continue to make glad the heart of childhood.
"Is There a Santa Claus?" Francis Pharcellus Church

As his family slept, the father stood barefoot
in his misbuttoned plaid pajamas, a wad of cash
gripped in his shaking left hand. Christmas Eve
booze screamed in his head. He wobbled
on the crest of the spinning Earth's curve,
a landlocked surfer hanging ten, swaying
and squinting, trying to read red names stitched
on the white tops of four stockings that hung
on the branches of the three globe pole light
that stood almost still. Slow dancing. Glowing.

Santa's helper cut in. Wiping his eyes, struggling
to recheck the list. Finally, his wife's name slid
slowly into focus. *Oh, Stella, sweet Stella,*
why you got to be so nice? Dontcha know, Santa
likes 'em naughty. He peeled off a few bills.
They fluttered, greenback butterflies, dancing,
diving, finally alighting on the soft white felt
that surrounded her name. From there, he coaxed
them down into the curve of her calf. *Next,*
ah, Janis, his daughter, a community college
freshman. *That Janis she gives a lotta lip.*
What a mouth. Good for her. A few bills took off
and flitted past her name. *Alan,* his eighth grade
son, *What a goody-two-shoes, too damn good.*
Hell, when I was his age, I fiddled in polka bands,
hung out in beer joints, drinking, smoking, chasing
broads. That kid needs to grow up. Ah nuts,
it's Christmas. A few more bills took off. His own
name snuck up and surprised him. *Albert, oh Albert,*
now that guy's a fucking saint! He slam dunked
the remaining roll into his ancient stocking
and then hung on its rim, steadying himself.
Once his balance returned, he ricocheted down
the hall, bouncing from wall to wall until he crash
landed face down on his bed. That night he slept
with one foot on the floor, an old trick to slow

the vertigo. Christmas morning came early. His nearly

grown kids were acting like kids, ripping paper, tearing
into the silence. They emptied their stockings,
where they found, for the first time ever, cash.
Their celebration grew louder. Albert roused
by the row trudged blindly into the room. His dead
weight fell back onto his recliner. Stella gave him
one of those looks and handed him his old stocking,
the same one he used as a depression era child,
one of five. He groped about its cracked body.
He felt the same old stuff that was always there—
a few oranges, some walnuts, a handful of coins.
Some Christmas, he thought, until he slid
his hand into the stocking's cool innards.
It hit a wad of paper. Puzzled, he pulled out
a payday's worth of cash. Dazzled, he let loose,
Holy shit Virginia, there is a Santa Claus!

Temperance

Each year come Ash Wednesday
my father swore off the sauce—
cold turkey for forty days
and forty nights of self-willed
sobriety. Our family's life
slid slowly off its hard edge.

Each night my parents watched
over my bedside Lenten prayers.
Finished, I'd climb into bed
and fall asleep counting
down the days until Jesus
would rise from the tomb
and the bottle would descend
from the unlocked cupboard again.

The Minors

The first reports from spring
training came north as we waited
for our buses on snow covered drives.
Baseball seemed a fantasy indeed.
We worried that the Yankees'
first month would be frozen out,
the Blue Jays might be snowed
under until June, but, gradually,
the land thawed. The red alcohol
in thermometers stretched up to fifty.

Suddenly, the girls in school
began to molt, sloughing off
thick coats and bulky sweaters,
and us boys began to spot the return
of white flesh and felt the flash
of our blood pulsing, brought
to a high boil by the spotting
of some sun-starved thighs
or the first sighting of a loose bra strap
migrating south down a slim bicep
out from the shoulder of a sleeveless shirt.

By the time opening day
rolled around, we needed
a diversion from life's mysteries
and our youthful ineptness
that kept us standing
in the on-deck circle—
a mile away from first base.
And so we rooted hard
for the teams of our choice,
too young yet to play
the real games of spring.

Lessons on Power

Each night by my parents' command,
I prayed to a plastic Jesus
who hung on a three inch wooden
cross. His size hid his pain.
There was little hint of sacrifice,
unlike the four foot Christ
who hung on the back wall
of the church and above us altar
boys as we worked—standing, kneeling,
ringing bells. I would tell myself
not to look up at those clenched shut
eyes, that oval mouth slightly opened,
that forehead lined with blood—
the color closer to brandy
than wine. I have never mastered
details in quick easy glances.

Each night after I signed
off—crossing myself, I stood
and crossed the room to turn
off the light. Above the switch
hung Carl Yastrzemski
four feet tall in full color, arms flexed,
full of power following through,
eyes looking up and out toward
left, following an unseen ball,
to where, sure as St. George, it slew
another humbled green monster.

Whiffle bat in hand
I stood toeing the sand
that washed into the drive
each spring. I held the classic
stance—hands head-high—
as the ball whistled in,
and on those rare pitches
when my cousin's curve did
not bite, and the yellow tube
said soundly, *The ball will clear
the cedar hedge in left,*
I knew the pose to strike. I hung

on the next generation's wall.

Last Sunday after watching my children
serve mass, I found myself in our garage
looking through boxes of ancient artifacts
packed away and moved a dozen times
since my youth. I happened across the poster
rolled, yellowed, and crumpled in the corner
of a battered U-Haul box. Yaz stood
there looking younger than I remembered,
holding the pose which is now forgotten
to all but us—the aging.

God's Radio

In Religious Ed a nun once told us that we
should always make the sign of the cross
before and after we prayed. The first gesture
opened God's wavelength, the second closed it off.

I wonder if the sister knew how many nights
I would lie in bed, panicked, wide awake
unable to remember if I had signaled
Roger and out. Odds or evens—heaven
or hell. I crossed myself without stopping,
hoping to land on evens or at least to interrupt
the feed before my memories of Linda Ursoni's
blouse and her fully developed fifth grade breasts
bubbled forth from the back of my pubescent mind.

Even as an adult, I find myself playing
the same game, while hoping that someday
I might cross myself one last time and be done
with it, but the deep need to hide always follows—
in the name of the Father, and of the Son. . .

Popcorn

I

My mother cooked batches of Jiffy Pop
on the kitchen stove. Their foil domes
swelled until my Mom, an RN by trade,
would perform culinary C-sections
that brought forth bursts of steam
and the sweet aroma of fresh popcorn.

On special summer nights, their contents
were split into four lunch bags. My sister
and I were put into our pajamas and then
into the back seat of the car. An old
dented cooler filled with iced soda and beer
rode between us as we drove to the drive-in
theater to watch a double feature of Disney
live action films. Us kids normally remained
awake through the first flick, but under blankets
with our heads propped on pillows, we'd nod
off not long after the intermission's dancing
hot dog did his number. Our folks didn't mind.

II

Excepting the National Geographic,
the first naked breast I ever saw
was huge, and it rowed up in a canoe.

We rarely went to real movies. Only
Saint Julie Andrews drew my family
to indoor shows. In *Hawaii,* the chaste
actress stood aboard a ship as natives
paddled out to welcome the missionaries
to their new positions. I noticed the greeters
wore flowers and no shirts. As they neared,
I learned that they weren't all men. My joy
over the scene ended as my mother's palm
landed squarely on my nose. My sister piled
on. Blinded by ten digits, I heard Mom
suggest that we all go get some hot popcorn.
My father wouldn't budge. From then on

every bare-breasted native brought on a form
of temporary blindness and a forced march
to the concessions stand. The marches slowed
as the natives began to adopt western ways
of dress. But at the point of the film where Saint
Julie was about to give birth, my mom
sounded the call, *Popcorn!* With a distended
stomach filled beyond its capacity with starch
and salt, I begged, *Please Ma, not again. No,
no more popcorn, please. . . .* As she dragged
me up the center aisle, strangers began to laugh
at this odd kid and his strange hunger strike.

III

The summer I graduated from high school,
back when boys could legally pretend
to be men by hanging on to their cans
of beer, a bunch of us decided to buy a case
of Utica Club and head down to the drive-in
which by then was trying to survive by showing
soft porn. We watched a fractured fairy tale
in which a bare and chesty woman screamed,
*Tell another lie. Oh yes, oh yes, Pinocchio,
tell another lie.* Our hearts raced as we sucked
our beers and tried to act cool, but the car's
fogged windows gave us away. I slipped out
into the night air and bought some popcorn.

Easy Magic

He sat entrapped by metal and plastic
waiting his turn. *These acts won't be hard
to follow.* Pictures of grandpas in ancient
uniforms, rusted medals, frogs tied in ribbons,
a book, a ball. *Big deal, I have a Mickey
Mouse napkin and a magic spell.*
He strained to stay in place.

The night before, he had turned seven.
Chocolate Mickey Mouse cake, candles
to blow out, presents to rip open, birthday
spankings endured from brothers and cousins,
a million perfumed goodbye kisses and his uncle,
the grown up kid, sitting in a corner. *Hey, Jase
want to see something great? I guess.*
The uncle took a paper napkin that sported Mickey's
image (an alpine rodent with a pointed hat)
and began to tear it into small pieces. *Big deal,
Frisky can do that, and he's a cat. Sure,
but can he do this?* The uncle's knuckles turned
white. He half sang some made up words and then
Presto. Slowly, a twin and earlier palmed
image of the mouse unfolded to a fairy tale's end.

Jeez, how'd you do that? Easy, it's magic.
For the next hour any paper product became fair game
for the entranced child. He folded and tore, cried
and swore. His mother glared at her brother. *Do
something!* she ordered. So the teenaged uncle
took his nephew to the child's room and promised,
*If you get in bed, I'll conjure up my magical
powers once again.* He gave the boy another napkin
and told him to tear it. Tired fingers went to work.
Now, squeeze and believe, said the man-child.
Jason's reserved effort wadded the napkin to a loose wad.
Here, let me help. The uncle secretly slid another folded
napkin between the boy's hands. The switch made,
the uncle instructed the boy, *Squeeze one last time.*
Then he told his clueless apprentice, *Now, unfold it.
Why? You'll see.* The first fold undone, no pieces
slipped or fell, another fold undone, all held fast. Faith

restored, the boy shook the image whole. He stared
at it, at his hands, at his art. *Why this time? Because,
that's the magic one. Now go to sleep.* The boy slid
between his sheets but never even blinked.

Jason, I said it's your turn. He began
the long march to the teacher's desk.
*I have a magic Mickey Mouse napkin
to share.* Oohs and teeters rose from the class.
He shredded the wizard's icon, chanted
his Uncle's chant, but the pieces
wouldn't knit. Horror-struck, he squeezed,
bent from the waist, lifted a foot—
earthquakes, volcanoes tremors
and hot tears shook his core.

Even the teacher had to laugh as she took
him by the shoulders and led his empty
frame back to his cold metal seat.
She pried his fingers open and removed
the wadded remains of a child's belief.

Leaving the Valley

I escaped my parents'
drunken rants by walking
the tracks that ran behind our house.
One evening I sat resting on the edge
of an old bridge. Built from hewn stones,
it stood just high and wide enough to allow
a wagon heaped with baled hay to pass
beneath. I dangled my worn canvas
high-tops above the dirt road's deep ruts.

A low rumbling, the stones
quaked, a freight train,
coming from nowhere fast,
spewing hot diesel fumes.
My head track-high swiveled.
The engineer laid on the whistle.
Trapped. I froze. The cars
leaned and swayed, passing
a foot above my fluttering
Yankee cap. I stared
at spinning steel, listened
to the rails' high-pitched tune,
whispered deep inside the thunder.

The iron storm passed, I sat
in a cold sweat taking in
the Mohawk Valley—rolling
greens fading to indigo—
until an overripe sun fell
through the molten horizon.
I watched the night's shadow
unfold and spread, pulling
itself toward the valley's rim.
As the landscape faded to black,
I knew I had to stand and leave.

I returned to find the house filled
with the television's blue glow
and blare. My mom and dad slept

it off in separate chairs. I closed
my bedroom door and dove
onto the bed. Sleep came fast.
I rested on the covers, fully clothed.

The Elk

Life's like that. . . .

"*The Moose,*" Elizabeth Bishop

Two days without a shower, decent food
or sleep, I ride squeezed into a blue
sweat-stale seat that reclines
into the ancient knees of the crank
who rides behind me. We have left
the driving to them, or at least
to the uniformed guy up front who
I pray is more awake than he looks.

I hoped to catch some sleep, but halfway
through the night, halfway home,
the crapper's busted door keeps banging
close, punctuating every bump, every
damned curve, keeping the beat of this
detoured run through the Twilight Zone,
banging out some Satanic lullaby near
the seat of a frazzled mother clutching
her frantic infant who miles ago forgot
how to cry. It now screams soul piercing
notes, well past the high range of any trained
diva. *Good God, what lungs.* The crank
moans. His wife counters, *What's the poor
mother to do?* He suggests, *She could cram
that kid's head into that damn door jamb
and kill two birds with one slam!*

An obese Elk of the highest order
rides next to me. He has spent his day
complaining, wishing that he had become
a Mason. *Kid, they take care of their own.
You don't find them riding no friggin'
Greyhound.* He paused his tirade often
and pulled a large flask from the breast pocket
of his beige corduroy blazer that must have fit
better when he bought it a few rutting seasons
back. Now deep into a drunken sleep, his bulk
oozes past his seat. He shifts pinning my shoulder
under the avalanche of his soft flesh. His head turns.
He snores his dragon breath into my melting face.

I tell myself that this is not the bus poem
I had hoped to live or write. Perhaps
mystical moose appear to hush quiet
conversations only on Canadian buses
on which Elizabeth Bishop rode and wrote.
This thought vanishes as the door slams,
the baby screams, the Elk's drooling head
kneads my shoulder. The hell-bound bus
swerves and fails to miss a suicidal skunk.
The cabin fills with a sickening odor.
Another mile toward our destination is gained,
for even at its most absurd, life's like that.

Punxsutawney Phil Forecasts
the End of the Romantic Period

In an early spring north of the Mohawk,
or in the late winter anywhere else,
we fifth graders stood in line behind our teacher
waiting to be fitted and shod with rented
snow shoes for a short field trip onto what was left
of the melting snow and then past the pine-lined
playground, through the naked maples and birches
down to the thawing yet frozen Nine Mile Creek.

In an early fall east of the Trinity,
or in a late summer anywhere else,
we sat behind our thick anthologies
opened to an assigned page, slouching
in long neat rows before our professor,
who expected to guide us through the poetry
of the long dead Romantics and Victorians
and given time, the more newly deceased
Moderns, while we earned three credits
and occupied time and an air-conditioned space.

Just past the tree line halfway to the creek
some of us boys spotted it first, a woodchuck
that wouldn't move. We yelled to our teacher,
Hey, over here. Panicked, he yelled back,
Don't! He slogged through the watery snow
with the rest of the class to where we stood
enthralled. *Is it dead?* someone asked. *No,
just playing possum,* some clown whispered.
As the nervous laughs died down, a timid suggestion
made its way through the pack. *Turn it over,
so we can get a better look.* The teacher,
figuring why not, used the tip of his snow shoe
to flip the stiffened corpse. At first, its yellow
bucked teeth held my eye, until the girls screamed
and some boys grunted, *Cool.* Then my eyes
were pulled down and found the pocket of maggots
swarming its exposed innards. Flustered, the teacher
suggested that we move on. Still, decomposition
remained the most impressive lesson we learned that day.

The professor read aloud each poem, and then once again,
stopping on certain words the second time through,
so he could point out the hand of genius that showed
through in the work's meaning and form. He lectured
on the nature of Aeolian harps and about the romantic romps
in which poets detected a benevolent yet unseen force.
I don't remember how it happened, but tiring of these dated
notions, something snapped. My hand, as if given life,
raised without my knowing, and then my voice was heard
for the only time that semester, and it was asking,
For all the time that these guys spent in the woods,
didn't they ever stumble across a dead and half-rotten
woodchuck? Our professor stared past me well out into space,
as if he was searching for the home planet of my alien
tongue. He then feigned an answer, shrugged and moved on.

Icarus Gets Summer Work

. . .it was not an important failure.
"Musée des Beaux-Arts," W. H. Auden

If you want to work with men, you need
to dress like a man. Here. The father
just up from the cellar handed the worn pair
of work boots that he kept for back ups
to his bookish son, who had just flown home
from his freshman year. The boy slid off
his sneakers and tried them on. He found
them at least a half size too big. At work
the next morning, he wore two pairs
of thick socks but still felt his father's
deep imprint beneath his feet.

The father landed his son the job, work
on a rural garbage route. Before the sun
rose on his first day, the kid learned
how to run the truck's hydraulic jaws.
He learned that handles were for amateurs.
Pros lifted garbage cans with the fore-edge
of their bent and gloved index fingers. This grip
allowed G-men to flip a can up to the truck's bin
where it would balance until he could step
under its end and shoulder it until the junk
fell out. The boy learned that since dents
will happen, he needed to ding each new can
so customers would learn to expect accidents.
As the day drew on, he learned to his disgust
that maggots resembled his mom's tapioca
and that there were sights and smells that could kill
an appetite. Most importantly he learned it paid
to work fast. The quicker the route was picked,
the sooner his workday would end.

He rode on the truck's rear running board.
A veteran of summers spent haying, the kid
knew how to jump from a moving platform.
To save seconds, he began to push his departures.
As the truck down shifted and slowed
at a remote farmhouse, he saw the brake lights
and jumped. He knew instantly that he was a slave

to velocity. He hydroplaned on worn soles
across the dew-soaked lawn. Hope flickered
as he began to run, but with each stride
his chin came closer to his knees
until he folded into a ball
and somersaulted forward
toward the one-three pocket
of the set out cans, and bam,

he rolled a perfect strike. Cans, trash,
papers, bottles filled the air. His head
ended up on the wet grass, his ass
came to rest on flattened and oozing bags,
his feet were propped on toppled cans.
As he waited for his breath to return,
and his head to clear, he stared through
spinning stars at his dad's Red Wings.
He heard the driver laughing, pounding
the dash while a Holstein stood across the road
eyeing him while calmly chewing her cud.

Blue Collar Poetics

Poetry is a way of taking life by the throat.
Robert Frost

I tell it like it is, my father's motto, a creed
he practiced in the image of his sect's
patron saint—Howard Cosell. As a boy I could
never see the point in being mean. I followed
the meeker men of the mike, the *homers*
and the comical *holy cowers*. The men my father
coldly dismissed. *Rizzuto's nuts! Bobby Murcer
couldn't even shine Mantle's or DiMaggio's shoes.*

Home on break from school, I rode
with my dad down to the nursing home.
My grandmother at ninety years plus, in poor
health, but as my father said *too damn stubborn
to die,* reclined in her bed, dried bones wrapped
in thin paper, kept together more by miracle
than sinew, the remnant of a hard woman
and even harder life. In her thick Lithuanian
accent she stared me down, her strangest grandson,
a grown man still in school. She complained
sharply with her keen tongue, *I had five children.
Five! I never thought I would find myself in such
a place. I always thought that at least one child
would care enough to share his roof with me.*

I began to look away when my father, her
youngest and least favorite son, a one time
delinquent turned dropout, turned merchant
seaman, turned union tin-knocker and distant
father, barked madly from his darkened corner,
*Jesus Key-riste Mary, you had five kids
because you had hot pants.* Holy cow!

The old bones gasped, and then suddenly
broke into a long-lost laugh. The three of us
guffawed, gasping for air, holding our sore guts,
as I wiped away hot tears and years of tact.

St. Peter's Square 1979

College kids half drunk on cheap spumanti,
we decided to stand at the barricades
for hours. As the crowd grew behind us
so did our plan. The new Polish Pope
was returning from Mexico and would pass
within earshot. We knew that he was known
to stop and bless or converse with pilgrims
who spoke his native tongue. Since my mother's
parents came from Poland, the group looked to me,
but my vocabulary was bluer than the Pontiff's
eyes. I feared my broken secondhand Polish
was more likely to land me in the bottom
of some secret and dank Vatican dungeon
than it was to gain us a Papal audience.

Plan B, we decided to consult our foreign language
pocket travel guide. Short of receiving the Paraclete's
gift of tongues, phonetics became our only chance.
We leafed through the little Polish it offered, looking
for some phrase that even Americans could pronounce.
Happy with our choice, we practiced in unison
as if we were again pre-communicants chanting
the *Baltimore Catechism* until we had it right.

That night as the young Pope rode past
a few feet away, we shouted in our best Berlitz,
Where are you going with our baggage?

The passing years bent the Pope
in half and hid him behind a cold
plastic mask, but I still relive that night.
Often in a dream, I see his confused look
snap around to our direction, and I swear
I can hear him answer, *Too far, my son, too far.*

Virgin Territory

The sun balanced
on the tip
of an ancient obelisk.

I sat cozied up
next to the woman
I had traveled

with through Europe
(my friend, my class-
mate, my groper,

my heavy petter,
my oral sexer
who was too Catholic

to be my lover)
breathing in her
skin and hair

there on the steps
of St. Mary Major's,
our Roman semester

nearly over. I fantasized—
saw the needle
pierce the ripe sun

which would remain
like an etherized scarab
suspended forever.

But the chaste star
rolled coolly down
behind the granite pin.

Stateside, my love
married an older man
she met soon after.

I read books, studied
poetry and the ache
of that horizon ungained.

Skeletons

As a kid I always found it harsh
when my mother claimed that if given
the chance to live her life over,
she'd become a cloistered nun.

My father, an old dog, loved to roll
in life's dirt. One night after I graduated
from high school, my bags packed for college,
he swayed up to me, a fresh Manhattan
sweating and sloshing in his hand. He offered
me slurred advise. *Kid, ya know if I could
do it all over again, I'd been an effing pimp.*

After returning from my semester abroad,
I handed out souvenirs. I gave my mom
water from Lourdes, a rosary blessed
by the Pope and a cheap t-shirt. I brought
my dad brandy from Spain, a Hofbrauhaus
half-liter stein, and second-hand accounts
of his World War II Pig Alley haunts.

My mother enjoyed her gifts, especially
her John Paul II t-shirt. He stood arms raised
and spread, glowing in black and white.
That it was two sizes too large didn't matter
to her. She wore it often and took to saying
again and again, *I can't believe how happy
the Pope looks.* My father, who believed
only to a certain point, finally broke one night
during our family meal. To her constant refrain,
he shot back, *For Christ sake, Stella,
I'd be ecstatic too if I had a tit in each hand.*
My mother looked down. The Pope looked
up, smiling, her breasts resting in his open palms.
She said nothing. I brayed and snorted, laughing
along with my bent and breathless dad.

A few days later, the shirt appeared, hanging
neatly in the corner of my closet. I didn't wear
it much and never in my mother's presence.

Remission

While shooting hoops
practicing for teams
I wouldn't make,
I pivoted, faked,
shot, followed through
and wished
she would die.
Follow your shot,
my instincts coached,
urged my frozen legs.
Still, I watched
the ball fall
free from the net.
Bounce, bounce
and roll away.

As a boy,
I was often ill.
Drowsy with fever,
my beaded head
would rest
in my mother's lap.
I remember
when the medicine
came, how she
raised my head
and pressed it gently
to her breast
which pulsed
and soothed
my ailing
chest and head.

Bed-bound
head shaven,
shriveled she lies.
Her pain
her drugs
I don't understand,
only her half-formed
words: *Jesus take me.*

Gaudy jewelry:
Rosaries, medals,
brown scapulars
adorn but do not comfort
her foreign shape.
Nor do I,
I only hide
my father's
razor blades.

Today, the basketball,
flat, covered by dust
lies hidden on some
garage shelf. She,
healed, but scarred
more than most,
finds some comfort
in knowing life
is the only sense
found in pain.
She sits quietly.
My nephew rests
nesting by her side.
Her paled hair and face,
the child's easy blond pose
confuse my senses,
and for one moment
I stare at my mother's
apparition nursing
my childlike ghost.

Reconciliation

Any true act of forgiveness participates
in the sacrament of Reconciliation.
Fr. Efren Nano

As a child I spent my days playing
self-invented games with baseball cards.
I transformed my mother's well-kept den
into a not-to-scale replica of Yankee Stadium.
The *house that Berecka built* consisted
of reassigned furniture. The afghan
covered sleeper couch became the bleachers
in deep center. The footrest of my dad's recliner
became the screen behind home plate,
the assorted cigar and shoe boxes
that housed my collection were arranged
in a semi-circle and became the outfield wall.
Four Nestea baseball coins—three of plastic
for the bags and one of tin for the dish—
were laid out three feet apart on the green
shag carpet. A brown ceramic ashtray
turned upside-down became the mound.

I rolled empty Hershey's Kiss wrappers
into game balls. After nine cards
took the field, I hummed the anthem.
Play ball! I knelt beside the plate,
a hitter gripped in my right hand.
I flicked a pitch with my left thumb.
The batter swung. Some men dribbled
slow rollers that died in the high infield grass,
others ripped frozen ropes into the gaps.
Still others, like Mickey Mantle, possessed
the great power to lift the ball deep, pulling
Ballantine Blasts beyond the Thom McAn box
that stood down the line in shallow right.

As I dragged the Mick around the bases,
he limped his home run trot. As he rounded
third, he tipped his helmet to me. After crossing
the plate, he shook hands with his teammates,
who lined up to welcome him back to their dugout
that sat below the bottom shelf of our coffee table.

My mom never saw the stadium,
its invisible white facade, never thought
our television resembled the monuments
in centerfield. She only saw the mess and grew tired
of working on the grounds crew, straightening
the chewed up field yet again. Like an ump
staring down an irate Ralph Houk, she warned me,
Clean up this junk, or it will all get heaved out.

And most of it did get tossed that day
my best sluggers decided to relax
out on the field between the games
of a regularly scheduled twin bill.

At first my grief paled and confused her,
but she regrouped to say, *Some lessons
are harder than others. Besides, son,
you were warned, and what's done is done.*

Still, I managed to keep a silent hope
that those cards had not been banned
but only suspended by a commissioner
whose punishments were known to be just.
Surely, she had thought this case through.
Once my lesson had been well learned, the Mick
and others would return from a secret place
to resume their careers. But as each birthday,
Christmas and Easter passed, I realized my cards,
like Gehrig and Ruth after their numbers
had been retired, were gone for good,

but not forgotten. When we were teens, my sister
bought me the *I'd be rich, but my mother threw out
my baseball cards* t-shirt, and I wore it everywhere.
One semester while in graduate school, I sold
my Roses and Carews to pay for books.
I couldn't resist reporting back that my Mantles
could have covered my tuition and fees as well.

By the time my son was playing Pokemon
games with cards that I failed to understand,
the baseball card market had crashed,

and I realized that belting tin foil balls
for home runs with my cardboard heroes
had done little to preserve their value.

They were worth even less that night as I sat
my watch next to her bed at the cancer hospice.
Sedated she mostly slept, so the sudden sound
of her voice shook me, but not nearly as much
as her words which offered the grace to absolve us
both. *Son, I'm sorry. . . those damned baseball cards.*

Leveling

Quietly, my father
and I worked,
leveling my mother's
fresh grave. We moved
in slow circles, raking
the broken earth flat.
We shook seeds
from handfuls of hay,
then covered the ground
with the straw that remained.

We didn't speak.
Nearly thirty years old,
I strained to stay
composed. I aped
his movements. I wanted
him to think that I
had become a man.

When we finished
filling and emptying
our watering cans,
my father, who cared
little for words, spoke
what I have come
to believe was his
greatest compliment:

Hey, kid,
don't forget
how to do this.

Leftovers

In an empty kitchen,
Thanksgiving dinner
over, the widower picks
meat from a spent carcass.

His daughters, mothers
themselves, meet behind
a locked bedroom door.

Their mother's jewelry
box lies open between
them as they sit
on their parents' bed.

They divide its contents,
heirlooms for their own
daughters, as they walk
the fine line between
blood and desire.

When they finish,
the family will
gather to eat
cold sandwiches
and desserts.

The Comic Flaw

The child is father of the man. . . .
"My Heart Leaps Up," William Wordsworth

OK, I give up. Life is not a joke.
To the thousands who have been kind
enough to point this out to me, thank you.
Although, if you guys had planned better,
called each other up, rented a big hall
and then performed an intervention,
perhaps it wouldn't have taken
forty-five years for this fool to somber up.

Looking back on my boyhood, I now realize
I was wrong to find it funny when my aunt
decided in her madness to become a cow,
to have giggled when she mooed or chewed
her food twice. I was way out of line
when I said that we should buy her a brass
bell or an automatic milking machine
for Christmas, and I apologize.

Nor was it funny when my idiot uncle John
dropped his birthday cake and took the accident
as an omen of his impending death that didn't come
for years. Later on that day, I was wrong
to play along when my father improvised
new lyrics for the Birthday Song which we all sang
full lunged, *It's curtains for you, it's curtains for you,*
it's curtains dear Jo-hn.... That we laughed
as he blubbered, blowing tear-filled breaths
at trick candles on the replacement cake
and then laughed even harder when the candles
flickered back was unforgivable, and I am truly sorry.

I now realize it wasn't amusing
when I had to pull my plastered father
out of the hall closet, the one by the john,
before he could piss on the round vacuum
again. Nor was it funny, or even ironic,
to be steering a Chevy down a country road
at the age of six, while my father
worked the pedals as he puked his guts

out of an opened window after proving
that he could hold his liquor yet again.

And you're right, it wasn't funny when I befriended
Napoleon, Hitler and Christ, with whom I loved
to talk baseball while I sat on the bench
outside the wing of the state hospital
where I waited to visit my strung-out mother
who got hooked on painkillers (long before Betty Ford)
by doctors who weren't able to diagnose the neuralgia
that seared her face and jaw for years.

No, you guys are right, but now
that I can't laugh at my childhood,
what am I supposed to do with it?

Legacy

The tray had hung for most of my childhood
near the stove and over our bread box. I gawked
at it while I choked down meals like kielbasa
and kraut. Under its framed glass sat the entrapped
wings of hundreds of butterflies arranged in chromatic
and concentric designs. This once-living mosaic
encircled a huge iridescent blue then purple
then Blue Morpho that dwarfed the small white
and yellow specimens which flitted through our yard.
I asked my dad often how something so strange
had come to land on our kitchen wall. The few times
he answered, he came alive and spoke of the war,
of the Merchant Marines, of how he spent Carnival
one year in Rio, what it was like to walk in a dream.

The black and white shot of my folks was taken
in a cocktail lounge on Broadway. They each wear
a broad smile and a suit. His tie wide and short
has slipped out beyond his buttoned jacket. She poses
at an angle, turns her head to the camera. They stand
apart, separated by the girth of a former champion,
the Manassa Mauler, Jack Dempsey. He towers
above them, arms encircling the young man and wife,
as he attempts a distant grin. A dapper middle-aged
businessman who's still trading on his hard-knuckled
past, he holds a half-smoked cigar in his large mitt
that rests on my dad's shoulder. The aging heavyweight
is centered by awed newlyweds, who are too young
to know what it's like to get knocked through the ropes
or to lose because a ref forgot to start the count.

After my mother died, my father told me *Go ahead.*
Take anything you want. He expected me to explore
the house, rummage through closets and her dresser
drawers, but I knew what I wanted, so I asked
for his Brazilian butterfly tray and that black and white
photograph snapped on their honeymoon. I was afraid
that I had asked for too much until my dad said, *Sure*
you can take that crap, but what do you really want?

Proof

At the post-reception wedding
party, an old friend of the bride's
father, Mr. Ostrowski was making
his way back to the open bar
when he overheard their debate.

A priest, holding a glass of port,
and a Holy Roller sat bickering
about the strength of the miracle
once conjured in Cana. The priest
held no doubts. The Lord's wine
was the Thunderbird of its time.
The Holy Roller knew Jesus
quenched the thirst of his guests
with virgin grape juice.

Everyone knew Mr. O,
a laid back brick layer,
a DP from post-war Poland.
He was always quick to give
a kind word which he wrapped
in his thick accent. But that night,
Bolek, who went by Bill,
froze solid with a look
emptier than his glass.
He spoke in a whisper
through a tightened throat:

Gott, you speak of Gott.
What do you know? I put
bodies into ovens, and, yet,
you speak of Gott.

The priest and the Holy Roller sat
agape, their faces paling to ash
as silence fell around them.

Beacons

Second semester freshman year,
we returned to our college lives
to learn that a classmate had died
in a crash while driving home.

Strangely, her roommate asked me to write a poem
about Patti and her death. Stranger still, I agreed.
The poem was well received. It is now lost to me.
I remember that it rhymed—all poems rhymed
when I was eighteen. No doubt it said that her death
had meaning constant with some cosmic theme.

These days I live below a rounded mountain—
the highest point in this depressed state
on which a lighthouse banned from Boston
Harbor sits. The step-daughter of a friend
who lives down the street died suddenly
last night while at a dance at Hoosac Valley High.
A neighbor called early this morning to let us know.
Done, I placed the phone back into its cradle,
slipped into my daughter's room where I watch her

sleep. Pad and pen in hand, this morning I write
a different poem, for the years have taught
me that at times like these, the relationship
between meaning and knowledge is not unlike
the tower on top of Mount Greylock and the State
of Massachusetts, who in times of hardship
extinguishes its beacon for budgetary reasons.

A Failure of Imagination

It's a cold late spring morning
as we set out upon our way.

Yippee yi-oh, yippee yi-ay.

We're heading through the Berkshires
my in-laws' house in Dallas three days
away, if this compact Chevy wagon
can herd these bald tires south.

Yippee yi-oh, yippee yi-ay.

My wife rides behind me, our daughter
pinned by her side. The kid's strapped
into her big girl booster seat. Braced for low
orbit, she holds fast to her newest toy.

Yippee yi-oh, yippee yi-ay.

It's a white Fischer-Price tape recorder
with a giant red microphone and karaoke
function, in which a tape of Fred Penner's
The Cat Came Back spins. Ghost Riders

in the Sky, *Yippee yi-oh, yippee yi-ay*

has locked her fancy and thrown away
the key. Amazing how adept a three year old
can become at rewinding a tape from the end
to the beginning of the same damn song.

Yippee yi-oh, yippee yi-ay.

Somewhere south of the Poconos, on edge
and dreading the next full-lunged chorus,
I decide to change the moment's diversion.
My nerves calm as my plan takes shape.

Yippee yi-oh, yippee yi-ay.

Rachael. My wife darts me that I-hope-

you-know-what-you're-doing look in the rear
view mirror. *Rachael.* She turns off the song.
I ask her how her invisible friend Elliot

is enjoying the trip. She blushes in horror,
screams, *Oh shit! We forgot Elliot.*
She demands that we turn around
and retrieve her abandoned companion.

With each southbound mile she cries louder.
Couldn't leave well enough alone, becomes
the constant chorus. Finally, an Interstate
rest stop welcomes us to West Virginia.

We pull in. My wife releases our soggy
child from a bucket full of tears and sweat.
Desperate, I carry her around the car, show
her our empty luggage racks. I say,

*You know that might be a good place
for an invisible dragon and friend to hitch
a ride.* Exhausted from her despair
Rachael claims she can see him sitting there.

Now relieved and after food and drink,
we pile back in for the trip's next leg.
As we try to pick up speed and merge
back into traffic, the four of us begin to sing

Yippee yi-oh, yippee yi-ay.

More than Bread

Here I am, at the HEB, stopgap
grocery shopping for my sick wife.
She handed me this list: Cheerios,
frosted blueberry Pop Tarts, chocolate
milk, Diet Coke, frozen pizzas
four cheese for the kids, another for us,
your choice, and DON'T FORGET
the Tylenol. I read it one more time.
I hear her voice, recorded in this
familiar long hand.
                I remember her
letters, when we were newly married
but living a country apart, split
between my new job and her old
contract. Her clothes moved in
a few weeks before she arrived.
I unpacked her garments, found
her scent, her shape. An easy task
yet I needed to pace myself. I ached.
Her closet filled.
                Some young mother
takes her eyes off stun, sets them to kill.
Excuse me, she says. I stand bellied
against a chest-high shelf, cereal boxes
pushed aside. My wife's list flipped.
My Foray precision point pen uncapped,
I scrawl on this blank side
                    and try to grasp
how these words—simple symbols, might someday
come to you, a reader I do not know. What they
might grow to mean.
                I jot my notes
about these miracles found without coupons
on aisle five, but I need to let this woman
get to her kid's favorite breakfast.
Besides, I'm wise enough to know
that I must find what I cannot forget.

Coming to Terms

My father's constant commandment
focused on my hair, which he
had confused with some household pet.
Train the damn thing. If you keep
it combed, it will learn to stay
in place. I listened to this heartfelt
yet blindly given advice again and again.

For close to two decades, I tried to keep
his law—*Keep thine hair combed,*
so it may learn to fall to the right,
but my hair had its own free will.
Its sense of order had been replaced
with one of wanderlust. Not even Daniel
could have tamed my wild mane,
nor could Moses, even with both arms
raised, have managed to keep it parted.

With oils, creams, and sprays,
my father anointed my head,
but my bad hair life went on,
until I was old enough to leave home.

Middle age has brought me comfort
with my hair, a chaotic mess
that hints at a more natural order
of things. My hair still falls where it may,
but before I take it on the three day
drive to my father's house, it mainly falls
on a barber shop floor. Some say
I have learned to use crew cuts
and ball caps to hide the truth,
but I prefer to see these simple acts
as humble sacrifices given in homage
to the most ancient of covenants.

My Life Among the Birds

My teenaged daughter raises three fingers
and turns her knuckles to me. She covers
her Texas twang with a fake New York accent
and tells me, *Hey, yuz da poet, Mister
Library-man, read between dees lines.*

I took bird watching in college, science credits
for my English degree. The flunk-out course
for biology majors, I took it on a lark
from the great protector of the golden
cheek warbler—a man with no sense
of humor. For lab exams he asked us
to identify eyeless, avian corpses stuffed
with cotton. Stumped often, I would write
down *dead bird* and plead for partial credit.

When my sister and I were small, we learned
never to make the same request three times
to our father. *Can we go? Hell, no. Please,
Dad? Go whistle. Aw, come on! Kiss
me.* He'd raise his extended middle finger
to his lips and blow us a mock kiss. As his
kids aged, we began to realize that flipping
the bird to one's children was less than normal,
so we'd invite our friends over and begin
to coax the birdman into his stale and profane
vaudevillian act to watch their shock and delight.

At the Aransas Refuge, the tower stands
forty feet high. Tourists flock up the concrete
ramps to reconnoiter the marsh, hoping
to catch sight of the whooping cranes.
Casual watchers often point out
graceful living semiquavers, bestowing
upon the common Great White Heron
celebrity status. The proud holder
of three credits in Avian Ecology,
I never correct them as they leave happy,
believing that their time has been well spent.

On this trip up north, I recall how my daughter

howled with laughter the first time she saw my
father flip me off. She now prides herself
on what she thinks is an artful imitation
of the old act. I have flown home by myself
to visit my recently stroke-stricken father. I sit
next to my sister waiting to learn the old man's
prognosis. The doctor enters and informs us
that the stroke has left him nearly blind
and has erased his vocabulary except for two words:
fuck and *no*. The doctor is taken aback
by our show of relief, so we explain that we
rarely, if ever, heard our father say anything else.

My Father's Passion

It's not hate
that crucifies
us, it's love

that pins us
down, creates
the willingness

to sacrifice—
like my old man
every morning

off to work, his
tin lunch bucket
in hand, climbing

into his rusted
junker to drive
into the city

for eight more
hours spent welding
stainless steel,

breathing noxious fumes
until he punched out
and drove back home

where he smoldered;
doused with beer, his
dimming eyes stared

square into another
day spent under
the hood, another

week shot, his pay
spent on her doctors
and on their kids

but not on the fishing

boat he talked
about until he

gave up, abandoned
such thoughts
and lost himself.

The Koans of Albert

What's the sound of one hand clapping?
An ovation at a live sex show. My old man
didn't know Zen from Shinola, but he loved
that joke. He often spewed his own blue sayings
that meant as little as the riddles the blind master
on Kung Fu assigned to his young Grasshopper.

When I tried to hand my father some line,
I often heard, *If bullshit was music,*
then kid, you'd be a brass band. If I said
that I had thought I had done something
which I had left undone, he'd blast back
You thought? You know what happened
to thought one day? It flew out your ass.

Success without effort brought forth higher
levels of nonsense. *Son, if you fell into a pile*
of shit, you'd come out smelling like a rose.
Or he might trot out his most surreal adage.
Kid, you're as lucky as a raped ape. I confess
that I meditated for long youthful hours,
trying to comprehend why a sexually assaulted
primate might be considered fortunate.
At first I thought the saying could be a primal nod
to Erich Von Daniken's alien chariot riders,
the horny spacemen who the Dane claimed
had relations with our hairy mothers,
deflowered apes who birthed the human race.
But if that was the case, it was the humans
and not the apes who gained from the exchange.
So I concluded the saying must be my blue
collar dad's secret wish to lead a bonobo's
work-free and sex-filled life. My father desired

most that I would become a big shot lawyer.
But this is where his profane and Zen-like
lessons backfired. For I now believe
that his koans were seeds that flew
from his ass and landed in a pile of bullshit
where roses and brass bands took root
and grew into a love of language that guided
his prize student into the poverty of poetry.

On Call

When I phone my old man,
he reports on the weather.
It's all the talk his stroke-
scrambled brain can muster.

Somewhere, behind his broken
synapses there's an army
of wise-assed comments
at the ready, like paratroopers
on D-Day waiting for the signal
to jump past his dentures, yell
Geronimo, and land by surprise
behind enemy lines. But their plane
just keeps circling, as they sit

there like my bored old man
on his recliner, watching the sun
set while noting the drop
in temperature, in case
his son calls this week.

Nature's Way

As a kid, when I first found
my father's soft porn magazines,
the sight of a woman's naked
full airbrushed breast made
my world spin, brought me
to some numb and ecstatic state.

Two college degrees, green eyes,
a love of poetry, but it was her breasts
I learned to love first. After twenty
years of marriage, my eyes still slip
from hers, fall to her chest. I cannot
tell you why, only that it is so.

Anthropologists will tell you
that my attraction, my obsession
with the breasts of the females
of my species is a learned behavior.

Chinese men once desired
the golden lotus, three inch
feet bound to perfection,
the object of centuries
of oriental erotica.

In some societies a glimpse
of thigh, the length of neck
delivers men deep into desire,
but what does it matter?

Does the bird know why
he sings, why he places
baubles in the lining
of the nest? Tricks

he may have learned
driven to school
by the desire
that always simmers
just beneath the skin.

Library Patrons and Conservation

The wild haired slightly crazed Jesus
Freak sat each day stinking mightily
behind a public access PC.
After tightening an ancient bicycle helmet,
he cruised the web, Googling for God,
the Holy Ghost and other matters of faith.

What he found he printed, mountains
of unbound paper that he squeezed
into plastic grocery bags. Each night
he pedaled off, balancing the extra
weight of his newly acquired knowledge.

One day while armored for action
he embarked on a cyber-quest
seeking visitations of the Virgin,
but other women came to call,
pop-up jezebels promising
to be hot, wet, and waiting just
for him. With the first click, Jesus
fell from his name. The Freak
now spends lost days in search
of free flesh or loudly banging
computer keys, combing for sex
in seedy chat rooms until closing.

Staff members have been directed
by our boss to let the Freak chat
since he now consumes much less
paper than prior to his conversion.

I often imagine the trees this command
has saved. In one I see a sated serpent
slackened on a thick limb eyeing
thankfully the darkly ripened fruit.

Styles of Reference

So Dad, why's the grass green,
or ice cold; why's the sun hot,
or the sky blue? To any question
that every child must ask,
my father, who was nothing
if not honest, always replied,
How the hell should I know?

Once when my son was four,
he rode strapped into his booster seat
as we drove home from daycare
and work. He asked me, *So Dad*
what's on the other side of space?

When I started school, my dad shelled
out big bucks that he didn't have
for two sets of the *Encyclopedia*
Britannica—the junior and senior
editions. From then on my questions
still met with his same plea of ignorance
to which he added, *Go look it up.*

I looked in the rearview mirror.
My son sat expectantly, as I fought
off years of training in flippancy.
Suddenly, struck by what I thought
was true inspiration, I answered
Heaven. Yes, son, I reckon heaven's
on the other side of space. I tossed
a glance at my son's framed
reflection. Surprised, I watched
his face sour. *Can't be,* he shot
back. *Why not? Because, Dad,*
then God would be too far away.
Trumped by a child's faith and out
of ideas, I promised I would try to Google
an answer as soon as we made it home.

Tutorial

Your. . . righteous indignation. . . must burn. . .
before you'll apprehend.

"*Possible Answers to Prayer,*" Scott Cairns

The community can't be kept out
of the community college library.
Tonight, I'm alone on the floor
when every known pita (library-speak
for pain in the ass) arrives as if to attend
some Problem-Patron Convention.
No name tags needed, I know them
all: Don, the scooter-bound ditto-head
who Googles the web for dirt on godless
pinko liberals while droning on and on
about his latest kidney stone. There's Ted,
the friendly Vietnam vet, who suffers
from panic attacks. Stable as a rusted
land mine, he reads anything he can hold
as he hangs on to the last shreds
of his frayed sanity. There's Big Hair,
the Queen of Mean who'd rather speak
in Spanish but bitches in English
whenever she's asked to follow a rule.
They and a dozen other oddballs
sit around me tonight, while students
work and study on their home computers.

When I was a kid, my mother insisted
that I be nice to everyone. Long before
politically correct Valentine exchanges,
she forced me to give each kid in my class
a silly card. I became the pied piper
of pariahs. Plagued by their constant
presence, I decided that these kids—
the retarded, the stupid the obese,
the thickly bespectacled, and those that suffered
from weak bladder control—were all so weird
that they couldn't be real. Rather, I came to believe
that they were only tests, placed on this earth to check
my manners. I enjoyed this flawed philosophy
until one night when I awoke to the cold realization
that I was far from being the coolest kid in school.

Ergo, I might not be real, but only my class president's
final exam. I couldn't sleep for weeks and learned
to harbor my thoughts in shallower waters.

Tonight as the library's walls close in,
I reconsider my primary school theory,
only to remember a line once penned by God
or Christ, or maybe it was Scott Cairns,
which states that my actions at this moment
toward this collection of irritating beings
will bring me closer or push me farther
from the Divine, a test which I fear
I cannot pass, so my tutors gather round,
patiently waiting for me to understand.

The Relic

After my mother took ill, my father
sought miracles. He bought large votives
that burnt each Sunday at the feet
of the patron saint of last resorts.
Each July he and I made the Saint Jude
novena that our less-than-rich Lithuanian
parish offered with the intention of remaining
solvent. The priest who needed help hoped
that I would be there to serve. If only
all prayers could be answered so easily.

After mass and a short prayer service,
the faithful and afflicted left their pews.
Some marched, while others limped
or shuffled, or were rolled toward us—
the priest holding the encased relic
and me holding a small piece of linen.
I tried not to stare at them—the deformed,
the goitered, the palsied, the blind,
the droolers—as they paraded to the open
altar gates to kiss the relic's glass
from which, with an unsteady hand,
I erased their lipstick and spit.

After her brain surgery, my mother
stayed in bed. Bald and bandaged,
she moaned low when not sleeping.
Aunt Helen, our family's religious
fanatic, dropped by the house on her way
back from Maryland and the shrine
of the newly canonized Mother
Seton. Helen glowed as she handed
my mother a small jewelry box.
I expected to see yet another medal
or rosary to add to the dozens my mother
wore or thumbed. She lifted the lid.
Her face fell into a blank stare. She thanked
Helen, handed me the gift, then slid down
her pillow and into a feigned sleep.
After my aunt left, I reopened the case.
Under a certificate of authentication,

I found a glass ball that held a dollop
of paste on which sat an affixed chip
of bleached bone. I found myself thanking
God for making me a whole sinner
and not a future and scattered Saint.

My mother died of an aggressive cancer
that ate her spine. Even when pumped morphine
did not touch her pain, she continued to pray,
a rosary twisted in her hand. After her funeral,
I left the Church and her capricious God.

I believed I would never return. When our daughter
reached first communion age, my wife, a Baptist,
reminded me of the cost we had agreed to pay
for our wedding in my then Church, a promise
to raise our children as Catholics. Thinking
back on my childhood, I decided my child
should have a chance to believe, so I found
myself begrudgingly attending Sunday Mass.
Then one week while going through the motions,
I found myself asking, *If my mother never
lost her faith, what right did I have to blame
her suffering for the death of my belief?*
At that moment I felt a small piece of faith affix
itself, and I began to pray that the glue might last.

For My Daughter as She Leaves Home

In my boyhood, I learned two legends—myths
about the Eucharist. In both tales a priest
loses faith, one while he walked to visit
the sick while carrying a host pressed
in the pages of his breviary. The other fell
into despair and doubt as he raised the wafer,
as he stood behind the altar at the moment
of consecration. When each looked again,
they found instead of bread, slivers of meat
centered in small pools of blood. The legends
state that scientists came to test the flesh
and in both cases found it to be human,
most likely extracted from a heart. Faith
returned to the priests. The transformed hosts
survive as relics, the objects of adoration.

I do not know what to think of these tales.
I find it hard to accept the miraculous.
Still, once you have moved on from here,
should you lose faith in your own worth
or in the fact that you are loved, I pray
that this cheap piece of paper on which I
have labored with my simple art might
become a sliver of my own certain heart.

Rural Mysticism

The road home out of Corpus
Christi leads through Gregory
and into the heart of San Patricio

County, where it cuts through
miles of cotton, corn and milo.
A divided highway, it runs

so straight that even past the posted
speed, steering seems an optional
act, allowing the mind to fall back

into itself, well past the radio,
past frequent glances into mirrors,
and out the passenger-side window

onto the young crops, where
no circles or other alien
epistles can be found.

Then, suddenly a side-
wise glance is timed to find
the angle of road and field aligned.

The crops begin to line up
and appear to open,
revealing endless rows.

The eye, baited then captured, is drawn
down these aisles, traveling expectantly
like a raptured mystic, closing

in on a glimpse of the infinite,
but soon the ideal view reshifts,
the paths vanish, the eye returns

back to the business of the road
and the unfinished drive back home
through a sea of unripened crops.

Meaning

It's only the second time in history we've had snow on Christmas, and it's the most in a 24-hour period. The last time was in 1918.
Larry Maifeld, National Weather Service,
Corpus Christi Caller-Times, December 26, 2004

Christmas Eve mass—
my kids serving,
my wife reading.
Barely Catholic,
I sit alone next
to the side exit,
on my mark, waiting
for the final blessing.

Amen. I race.
First to the door,
a half-step out.
Snow. Snow
falling, dancing,
reflecting lights,
filling the night,
coating cars, palm
trees, everything.

It's snowing,
I let slip.
The guy two steps
back laughs.
I hold the door,
then walk on.
He says,
It's snowing.
The guy behind
him laughs. . . .

One by one,
the church empties
out into belief.

I stand grinning.
Joined by my family,

giddy, we watch
as miracle
upon miracle
silently piles up.

Commuting

How far can a fog lift
before it becomes a cloud?

Whatever it was, it hung
above the causeway
a few feet above each car
and truck, as we drove
over the shallow end
of the Gulf, consumed
with the needs
of our daily commute.

I noticed how the gulls
and pelicans disappeared
diving up into the thickness
but thought little of it, until
I rounded the long curve
near the final exit,
and there it hung
like a shroud, completely
obscuring the upper two-thirds
of the Harbor Bridge.

While being pulled along
by the constant traffic,
I watched the countless
sets of tail lights
ascending into obscurity,
taking on faith that beyond
it still lies the bridge
into the city of Corpus Christi.

In Dwelling

Listen to the Buddha,
or to the Christ.
They will tell you
that inside of you
there exists a universe,
the kingdom contained,
within the divine spark
inside the big bang
of the heart.

Each Sunday my parents dragged us
to God's house, and there he stood,
bald with shocks of white. His large head
rested on a rotund frame. He prayed
in Latin, preached in Lithuanian.
Eventually, I was set straight and learned
he was just an unkempt Franciscan,
a keeper of rites, a preacher of the way.
As I grew, I began to serve and learned
which candles to light, when to ring
the bells and the guilty buzz that came
with stolen sips of unconsecrated wine.

When our priest died
at the altar during the Easter Vigil,
my middle school world quaked.
At his wake, they laid him out
in the church, coiffed and clean,
his face, ashen and foreign.

That night, I lay
in bed on my back,
the covers up to my chest,
on which I rested
my folded hands.
I saw myself
in his place. My mind
caught, locked
on one word
—death.
All went dark.

I stepped
and fell
into my chest—
an abyss—
endlessly falling,
spinning, speeding
deeper into an endless
darkness. Breathless,
panicked, I rolled
into a ball, fought to come
to. I returned fevered,
soaking wet. I never slept
on my back again.

Thirty years removed from that night,
I dream that I return to the place
of the void. My heart begins to rev,
as I fall, but then the darkness pales,
and I come to rest in a garden bordered
by an endless sea filled with grace—
a deep sanguine wine. A hot breath
finds my nape and then a tap lands
on my shoulder. Uneasy, I turn to find
my old priest holding two gold cups
which he fills with the tide at our feet.
He smiles, hands me a chalice,
and says, *There's plenty. Let's drink.*

Acknowledgements

Poems, some in altered forms, have appeared in these journals, collections and anthologies: *Windhover, Red River Review, Ardent, New Texas, Oklahoma Review, The Christian Century, American Literary Review, MO: Writings from the River, Slow Trains, Penwood Review, Windward Review, Concho River Review, Octopus Beak Inc.*, *Each Man has One Life* (Trilobite Press, 2004), *Beacons* (Oil Hill Press, 2007), *Mountain Time* (Old Mountain Press, 2005), *Two Southwests* (VAC, 2008).

LaVergne, TN USA
24 February 2011
217855LV00001B/76/P